Sun Time Snow Time

First published 2013 by A & C Black,
an imprint of Bloomsbury Publishing Plc
50 Bedford Square
London WC1B 3DP

www.bloomsbury.com

Copyright © 2013 A & C Black
This collection copyright © 2013 Grace Nichols
Come on into my tropical garden © 1988 Grace Nichols
Give Yourself a Hug © 1994 Grace Nichols
Illustrations copyright © 2013 David Dean

The right of Grace Nichols and David Dean to be identified
as the author and illustrator of this work has been asserted
by them in accordance with the Copyrights, Designs and
Patents Act 1988.

ISBN 978-1-4081-9300-6

A CIP catalogue for this book is available from the British Library.

Printed and Bound by CPI Group (UK) Ltd,
Croydon CR0 4YY

1 3 5 7 9 10 8 6 4 2

MIX
Paper from
responsible sources
FSC® C020471

Sun Time Snow Time

A poetry collection by Grace Nichols
Illustrated by David Dean

A & C BLACK
AN IMPRINT OF BLOOMSBURY
LONDON NEW DELHI NEW YORK SYDNEY

Contents

Foreword

Children often ask me where I get my ideas for writing poems. Ideas come from all around: from things remembered vividly from my childhood; from the natural landscape of creatures and happenings all around me; from things people say; from mythology and dreams; and of course from reading books.

You could say my imagination was first awakened by tropical things, as my early childhood (up to the age of eight) was spent in a small village along the Atlantic coast of Guyana, in South America. Whenever it rained heavily our yard became flooded, and one of the best memories I have of myself as a child is standing in rippling sunlit brown water and watching the shapes of fish go by below the surface. Poems are a bit like fishes to me; each complete in itself, carrying its own living mystery and symmetry.

The rest of my childhood was spent in Guyana's capital, Georgetown, where we'd moved to. I joined our 'Public Free Library' and was a regular bookworm. Among my favourite books were the 'William' books by Richmal Crompton. They made me laugh out loud. I also dipped into my father's books of poetry (mostly English poets such as Keats, Wordsworth, Christina Rossetti). I've always been moved by the music and the image-making power of words.

In *Come on into my tropical garden*, my first book of poems for children, published 25 years ago, I tried to capture something of that bright hot 'floody' world of the village I grew up in, and something of the everyday speech of the people, which we call 'creole'. Creole is a mixture of English words with the rhythms and bits of the languages of the different people who make up the Caribbean: African, Asian, Amerindian, European, a kind of rich 'cook-up'.

My second book of poems for children, *Give Yourself A Hug*, was very much inspired by life in England and especially by the weather – crunching through thick powdery snow, helping my daughter to make a snowman, picking blackberries, and just observing life in general. I've been living in England for over thirty years now, longer than I lived in Guyana, which used to be a British colony.

As these first two children's books were out of print, we thought it a good idea to bring them back together again, embracing both worlds with a new name: *Sun Time Snow Time*. I hope you enjoy reading them.

And one piece of advice...

If you should ever find yourself writing a poem, remember to be true to your imagination. Trust the first picture or image that comes to mind. It often holds the key to unlocking the whole poem. Remember that the first line that comes to you doesn't always end up being the first line in the finished poem. It might end up being the very last line.

Grace Nichols

About the Author

Grace Nichols was born in Guyana and came to Britain in 1977. She has written many books for both children and adults and reads her work widely across England and internationally. Her awards include the Commonwealth Poetry Prize and the Guyana Poetry Prize as well as a Chomondeley Award. Her *Paint Me A Poem* (A&C Black) was named the Children's Poetry Bookshelf Best Single Author's Collection. Her children's collections include *The Poet Cat* (Bloomsbury) and *Everybody Got a Gift* (A&C Black). She has also edited anthologies for younger readers. She was poet-in-residence at The Tate Gallery, London 1999–2000.

Grace Nichols lives in Sussex with her husband, the poet John Agard. She has two daughters.

Sun Time

Poems from *Come On Into My Tropical Garden*

Come on into my Tropical Garden

Come on into my tropical garden
Come on in and have a laugh in
Taste my sugar cake and my pine drink
Come on in please come on in

And yes you can stand up in my hammock
and breeze out in my trees
you can pick my hibiscus
and kiss my chimpanzees

O you can roll up in the grass
and if you pick up a flea
I'll take you down for a quick dip-wash
in the sea
believe me there's nothing better
for getting rid of a flea
than having a quick dip-wash in the sea

Come on into my tropical garden
Come on in please come on in

12

Alligator

If you want to see an alligator
you must go down to the muddy slushy end
of the old Caroony River

I know an alligator who's living down there
She's a-big. She's a-mean. She's a-wild.
She's a-fierce.

But if you really want to see an alligator
you must go down to the muddy slushy end
of the old Caroony River

Go down gently to that river and say
'Alligator Mama
Alligator Mama
Alligator Mamaaaaaaaa'

And up she'll rise
but don't stick around
RUN FOR YOUR LIFE

I Like to Stay Up

I like to stay up
and listen
when big people talking
jumbie stories

I does feel
so tingly and excited
inside me

But when my mother say
'Girl, time for bed'

Then is when
I does feel a dread

Then is when
I does jump into me bed

Then is when
I does cover up
from me feet to me head

14

Then is when
I does wish I didn't listen
to no stupid jumbie story

Then is when
I does wish I did read
me book instead

'Jumbie' is a Guyanese word for 'ghost'.

15

Moon-Gazer

On moonlight night
when moon is bright –

Beware, Beware,
Moon-Gazer man
with his throw-back head
and his open legs –
gazing, gazing up at the moon –

Moon-Gazer man
with his seal-skin hair
and his round-eye stare –
staring, staring
up at the moon

Moon-Gazer man
standing tall
lamp-post tall
just gazing up
at moon eye-ball

But never try to pass
between those open legs
cause Moon-Gazer man
will close them with a snap –
you'll be trapped

Moon-Gazer man
will crush you flat.
Yes, with just one shake
suddenly you'll be –
a human pancake

On moonlight night
when moon is bright
for goodness sake
stay home – and pull
your window curtain tight.

*Moon-Gazer is a supernatural figure in Guyana, an
extremely tall man, usually seen straddling roadways
on moonlit nights. It's best to avoid passing between
his open legs.*

They Were my People

They were those who cut cane
to the rhythm of the sunbeat

They were those who carried cane
to the rhythm of the sunbeat

They were those who crushed cane
to the rhythm of the sunbeat

They were women weeding, carrying babies
to the rhythm of the sunbeat

They were my people working long ago
to the rhythm of the sunbeat

They were my people with scars to show
rising-up to the rhythm of the sunbeat.

Poor Grandma

Why this child
so spin-spin spin-spin
Why this child
can't keep still

Why this child
so turn-round turn-round
Why this child
can't settle down

Why this child
can't eat without getting
up to look through window
Why this child must behave so

I want to know
Why this child
so spin-spin spin-spin
Why this child can't keep still.

Riddle

Me-riddle me-riddle me-ree
Me father got a tree
Tell me what you see —

It's big
it's rough
it's hanging high
Came with old Captain Bligh
From way across the sea

You can bake it
You can boil it
You can roast it
You can fry it
Or find it in a dish of flying-fish —

Still can't guess?
Well add bread to fruit
And you'll get the green truth
Of this riddle
Which is simply — a breadfruit

Granny Granny Please Comb my Hair

Granny Granny please comb my hair
you always take your time
you always take such care

You put me on a cushion
between your knees
you rub a little coconut oil
parting gentle as a breeze

Mummy Mummy
she's always in a hurry-hurry rush
she pulls my hair
sometimes she tugs

But Granny
you have all the time
in the world
and when you're finished
you always turn my head and say
'Now who's a nice girl'

Cat-Fight

Spitting
    and spurring
clawing
    and furring
wailing
    and railing
shrieking
    and tearing
hissing
    and scratching
snarling
    and snatching
bawling
    and mauling
Man, it's really appalling –

Granny throw a bucket of water, please.
I can't stand the sound of all that caterwauling.

My Cousin Melda

My Cousin Melda
she don't make fun
she ain't afraid of anyone
even mosquitoes
when they bite her
she does bite them back
and say –
'Now tell me, how you like that?'

Wha Me Mudder Do

Mek me tell you wha me Mudder do
wha me mudder do
wha me mudder do

Me mudder pound plantain mek fufu
Me mudder catch crab mek calaloo stew

Mek me tell you wha me mudder do
wha me mudder do
wha me mudder do

Me mudder beat hammer
Me mudder turn screw
she paint chair red
then she paint it blue

Mek me tell you wha me mudder do
wha me mudder do
wha me mudder do

Me mudder chase bad-cow
with one 'Shoo'
she paddle down river
in she own canoe
Ain't have nothing
dat me mudder can't do
Ain't have nothing
dat me mudder can't do

Mek me tell you

Moody Mister Sometimish

Mister Sometimish, Mister Sometimish
you too sometimish!

Sometimish you tipping you cap
with a smile

Sometimish you making you face
sour like lime

Sometimish you stopping in for a chat
Sometimish you passing just like that

Sometimish you saying 'how-dee' and you waving
Sometimish you putting your head straight
you playing you ain't hearing
when I calling you
but Mister Sometimish I can be sometimish too
because you too sometimish, Mister Sometimish
Man you too sometimish.

Mango

Have a mango
sweet rainwashed
sunripe mango
that the birds themselves
woulda pick
if only they had seen it
a rosy miracle
Here
take it from mih hand

Banana Man

I'm a banana man
I just love shaking
those yellow hands
Yes, man
Banana in the morning
Banana in the evening
Banana before I go to bed
at night – that's right
that's how much I love
the banana bite

I'm a banana man
not a superman
or a batman
or a spiderman
No, man
Banana in the morning
Banana in the evening
Banana before I go to bed
at night – that's right
that's how much I love
the banana bite

Drinking Water-coconut

Feeling thirsty
feeling hot?
Nothing to cool you down
like a water-coconut

With a flick of her cutlass
market-lady will hand you —
a whole little world
with a sweet hole brimming on top
when you put it to your head
you won't want it to stop

Then you'll be wondering
if there's jelly inside
ask market-lady she wouldn't mind
she'll flick the coconut right open for you
she'll flick you a coconut spoon
to scoop with too

Feeling thirsty
feeling hot?
The best thing to spend yuh money on
is a water-coconut.

Mama-Wata

Down by the seaside
when the moon is in bloom
sits Mama-Wata
gazing up at the moon

She sits as she combs
her hair like a loom –
She sits as she croons
a sweet kind of tune

But don't go near Mama-Wata
when the moon is in bloom
for sure she will take you
down to your doom.

Star-Apple

Deepest purple
or pale green white –
star-apple is a sweet fruit
with a sweet
star-brimming centre
and a turn-back skin
that always left me –
sweetly sticky mouth

Early Country Village Morning

Cocks crowing
Hens knowing
later they will cluck
their laying song

Houses stirring
a donkey clip-clopping
the first market bus
comes jugging along

Soon the sun
will give a big yawn
and open her eye
pushing the last bit of darkness
out of the sky

The Sun

The sun is a glowing spider
that crawls out
from under the earth
to make her way across the sky
warming and weaving
with her bright old fingers
of light

Sky

Tall and blue
true and open

So open my arms have room
for all the world
for sun and moon
        for birds and stars

Yet how I wish I had the chance
to come drifting down to earth –
        a simple bed sheet
covering some little girl or boy
just for a night
        but I am Sky
        that's why

I am the Rain

I am the rain
I like to play games
like sometimes
      I pretend
I'm going
      to fall
Man that's the time
I don't come at all

Like sometimes
I get these laughing stitches
up my sides
      rushing people in
and out
      with the clothesline
I just love drip
      dropping
down collars
      and spines
Maybe it's a shame
but it's the only way
I get some fame

Honey-B Bottle

Honey-B Bottle
B-Bottle
Honey-B Bottle

Hear the children cry
as the old bottle-man,
pushing his cart,
passes slowly by:

'Big bottles, small bottles,
flattie bottles, round bottles,
green bottles, brown bottles,
drinks bottles, rum bottles,
Bottles I buy, bottles I buy,
bring them wet or dry,'

Honey-B Bottle
B-Bottle
Honey-B Bottle

Hear the children cry.
And reason they call him
'Honey-B Bottle'
is clear for all to see –

It's because he likes
the fat round bottles best
where the honey use to be.
And, for them, pay an extra penny.

Lizard

A lean wizard –
watch me slither
up and down
the breadfruit tree
sometimes pausing a while
for a dither in the sunshine

The only thing
that puts a jitter up my spine
is when I think about
my great great great
great great great great
great great grandmother
Dinosaura Diplodocus

She would have the shock of her life
if she were to come back
and see me reduced to lizardsize!

Dinosaurs

Diplodocus
Brontosaurus
Tyrannosaurus
Fabrosaurus

How I love the sound of dinosaurs
How I love their mighty jaws
and their mesozoic-claws

Dinosaurs O Dinosaurs
you might have been ferocious
but what a loss!

One hundred million years ago
you were the boss

Cow's Complaint

Somebody calls somebody
a lazy cow
now in my cow's life
I ask you how?

If it wasn't so unfair
I would have to laugh
Dear children, as it is
I can only ask

Who gives you the milk
for your cornflakes
(crispy crunchy yes)
but it's my nice cold milk
that really brings them awake
children make no mistake

Who gets up at the crack of dawn
and works until the set of sun
Who eats up the grass
helping to mow the place for free
tell me who if it isn't me

Who gives you hamburgers
Who gives you steaks
it's my meat they take
it's my meat they take

    So the next time
    you call anyone a lazy cow
    think again, my friend, you'd better
    especially if your shoes are made of leather

The Fastest Belt in Town

Ma Bella was the fastest belt in town
Ma Bella was the fastest belt
for miles and miles around

In fact Ma Bella was the fastest belt
both in the East and in the West
nobody dared to put Ma Bella to the test

plai-plai
her belt would fly
who don't hear must cry

Milk on the floor
and Ma Bella reaching for – de belt

Slamming the door
and Ma Bella reaching for – de belt

Scribbling on the wall
and Ma Bella reaching for – de belt

Too much back-chat
and yes, Ma Bella reaching for – de belt

plai-plai
her belt would fly
who don't hear must cry

Ma Bella was the fastest belt in town
Ma Bella was the fastest belt
for miles and miles around

In fact Ma Bella was the fastest belt
both in the East and in the West
nobody dared to put Ma Bella to the test

Until one day
Ma Bella swished, missed
and lashed her own leg

That was the day Ma Bella got such a welt
That was the day Ma Bella knew exactly how it felt
That was the day Ma Bella decided to hang up her belt.

Old Man's Weary Thoughts

Sun – too much sun
Rain – too much rain
Grass – too much green
Sky – too much blue
'Lord, dis world
ah weigh me down fuh true!'

Parakeets

Parakeets wheel
             screech
                    scream
in a flash of green
among the forest trees
sunlight smooth their feathers
cool leaves soothe their foreheads
creeks are there for beaks
lucky little parakeets

I'm a Parrot

I am a parrot
I live in a cage
I'm nearly always
in a vex-up rage

I used to fly
all light and free
in the luscious green
forest canopy

I miss the wind
against my wing
I miss the nut
and the fruit picking

I am a parrot
I live in a cage
I'm nearly always
in a vex-up rage

I squawk I talk
I curse I swear
I repeat the things
I shouldn't hear

So don't come near me
or put out your hand
because I'll pick you
if I can
pickyou
pickyou
if I can

I want to be Free
Can't You Understand

Doctor Blair

Doctor Blair is the name of a bat
In the forests of Guyana they call him that –

Cause Doctor Blair has a winging flair
for visiting his patients in the dead of night –
Doctor Blair with his surgical flaps
and his little black-sac tucked under his back

Even if you don't want to see him
Doctor Blair makes his rounds
and he comes without as much as a sound
to perform a pain free operation

Yes, while you're asleep
his appointments he'll keep –
in the morning all you'll see
on your leg is a thin line of blue –

Where the blood seeped through
Where the blood seeped through

*Remembering Oliver Hunter, Guyana man and
one-time pork knocker, who told me about Dr Blair.*

For Forest

Forest could keep secrets
Forest could keep secrets

Forest tune in every day
to watersound and birdsound
Forest letting her hair down
to the teeming creeping of her forest-ground

But Forest don't broadcast her business
no Forest cover her business down
from sky and fast-eye sun
and when night come
and darkness wrap her like a gown
Forest is a bad dream woman

Forest dreaming about mountain
and when earth was young
Forest dreaming of the caress of gold
Forest rootsing with mysterious Eldorado

and when howler monkey
wake her up with howl
Forest just stretch and stir
to a new day of sound

but coming back to secrets
Forest could keep secrets
Forest could keep secrets

And we must keep Forest

49

Sea Timeless Song

Hurricane come
and hurricane go
but sea – sea timeless
sea timeless
sea timeless
sea timeless
sea timeless

Hibiscus bloom
then dry wither so
but sea – sea timeless
sea timeless
sea timeless
sea timeless
sea timeless

Tourist come
and tourist go
but sea – sea timeless
sea timeless
sea timeless
sea timeless
sea timeless

Crab Dance

Play moonlight
and the red crabs dance
their scuttle-foot dance
on the mud-packed beach

Play moonlight
and the red crabs dance
their side-ways dance
to the soft-sea beat

Play moonlight
and the red crabs dance
their bulb-eye dance
their last crab dance

Snow Time

Poems from *Give Yourself a Hug*

Morning

Morning comes
    with a milk-float jiggling
Morning comes
    with a milkman whistling
Morning comes
    with empties clinking
Morning comes
    with alarm-clock ringing
Morning comes
    with toaster popping
Morning comes
    with letters dropping
Morning comes
    with kettle singing
Morning comes
    with me just listening.
Morning comes to drag me out of bed
— Boss-Woman Morning.

Sun Is Laughing

This morning she got up
on the happy side of bed,
pulled back the grey sky-curtains
and poked her head
through the blue window
of heaven,
her yellow laughter
spilling over,
falling broad across the grass,
brightening the washing on the line,
giving more shine
to the back of a ladybug
and buttering up all the world.

Then, without any warning,
as if she was suddenly bored,
or just got sulky
because she could hear no one
giving praise
to her shining ways,
Sun slammed the sky-window close
plunging the whole world
into greyness once more.

O Sun, moody one,
how can we live
without the holiday of your face?

Feeling Hungry

When you're feeling hungry
time can go by so slowly,
like when I'm out shopping with Mum.

I say, 'I'm hungry'
she says, 'You've just eaten'

I say again, 'I'm hungry'
She says again, 'You've just eaten'

'But I'm still hungry'
'But you've just eaten!'

'Well I don't know, it must be the cold
but me belly feel like a dough-nut with a hole.'

Me and Mister Polite

Again and again
we met in the lane.

We met in the sunshine
We met in the rain
We met in the windy
We met in the hail
We met in the misty
And autumn-leaf trail
On harsh days and dark days
On days mild and clear

And if it was raining
He'd say, 'Nice weather for ducks'
And if it was sunny
He'd say, 'Good enough for beach-wear'
And if it was windy
He'd say, 'We could do without that wind'
And if it was nippy
He'd say, 'Nippy today'
And if it was cold-windy-rainy-grey
(which it nearly always was)
He'd say, 'Horrible day'
Or 'Not as good as it was yesterday'

And he'd hurry away with a brief tip of his hat
His rude dog pulling him this way and that.

First Spring

You know that winter's almost gone
when you step outside and feel
the first warm fingers of the sun
touching your back,
like a hesitant friend.

You know that winter's almost gone
when you walk around
and suddenly, in the back garden —
a posse of daffodils
nodding to the earth's sweet hum.

Now you're running out the gate
Now you're running . . . down the pave
There's a shout in your wave
There's a skip in your sing —

First day of spring.

Daffodils

Long-neck ones
Yellow swans
Too soon gone.

For Dilberta
Biggest of the elephants at London Zoo

The walking-whale
of the Earth kingdom – Dilberta.

The one whose waist
your arms won't get around – Dilberta.

The mammoth one whose weight
you pray, won't knock you to the ground.

The one who displays toes
like archway windows,
bringing the pads of her feet down
like giant paperweights
to keep the earth from shifting about.

Dilberta, rippling as she ambles under
the wrinkled tarpaulin of her skin,
casually throwing the arm of her nose,
saying, 'Go on, have a stroke'.

But sometimes, in her mind's eye,
Dilberta gets this idea – She could be a Moth!
Yes, with the wind stirring behind her ears,
she could really fly.

Rising above the boundaries of the paddock,
Making for the dark light of the forest –

Hearing, O once more, the trumpets roar.

Roller-Skaters

Flying by
on the winged-wheels
of their heels

Two teenage earthbirds
zig-zagging
down the street

Rising
unfeathered –
in sudden air-leap

Defying law
death and gravity
as they do a wheely

Landing back
in the smooth swoop
of youth

And faces gaping
gawking, impressed
and unimpressed

Only mother watches – heartbeat in her mouth

My Gran Visits England

My Gran was a Caribbean lady
As Caribbean as could be
She came across to visit us
In Shoreham by the sea.

She'd hardly put her suitcase down
when she began a digging spree
Out in the back garden
To see what she could see

And she found:
That the ground was as groundy
The the frogs were as froggy
That the earthworms were as worthy

That the weeds were as weedy
That the seeds were as seedy
That the bees were as busy
as those back home

And she paused from her digging
And she wondered
And she looked at her spade
And she pondered

Then she stood by a rose
As a slug passed by her toes
And she called to my Dad
as she struck pose after pose,

'Boy, come and take my photo – the place cold,
But wherever there's God's earth, I'm at home.'

Listening To My Big Sister's Denim Rave

My fashion-saviour
My shelter-in-a-storm,
the number in which
I can't go wrong.

No matter the fray
No matter the rip
No matter the creases
No matter the split

Just watch me slip/zip/trip
In my old denims.
Watch me slide/stride/glide
In my old denims.
Watch me dance/prance
As I advance in my old denims.

Yes, when I need a bit
Of street-cred style –
Can't beat my old denims
At the bottom of the clothes-pile.

In With The Rhythm

In with the rhythm
In with the swing
In with the mood
Of the laser-lightning

      Music the finder
      of the chord in my brain
      Music the magic that takes
      away my homework-strain
      Music the maker that makes
      all movement come unchained

Turn up the volume
And close the door
Music, make tidy
My bedroom floor

'Summer Is Hearts' Says Sammy Selvon

skies bluer
larks truer

sun golder
folks bolder

leaves lusher
bees buzzer

grass deeper
fruits sweeter

'Summer is hearts' says Sammy Selvon,
munching his slice of water melon.

Berries

Strawberry

You wear your heart
on the edges
of your green sleeves,
hanging small and red,
close to the fields,
Strawberry –
studded with tiny seeds
of love.

Blackberry

Velvet pouch
of sweetness
this is true –
We have to prick hands
to get you.

Raspberry

It's the rasp
in your berry
that makes us tick.

It's the tang
in the flavour
that gives us a kick.

But raspberry
why does one of
your tiny pulps – all aglow

Remind me so
of a full-blooded
mosquito?

Mister Goodacre's Garden

The neighbours say he's weird and wicked
Just cause Mister Goodacre won't mow down
His high grass or thicket,
(Their own lawns look ready
for billiards or cricket)

I guess he just loves tall grass waving
I think the length of his dandelions amazing,
But the neighbours keep throwing him these
spearing-looks,
Which seem to say, 'You're lowering the tenor
Of the neighbourhood.'

Mister Goodacre just stands there
Whistling carefree,
Waving a water-gun for all to see;
'Think me lazy,' he says, 'think me crazy,
But I will defend my dandelions and daisies'.

More power to your wild flowers, Mister Goodacre,
But while you're basking . . .
I'm afraid the neighbours
Are planning a grass-murder
With their lawn-mowers.

Counting Sleep

I've tried counting sheep
even goats that bleat and frogs that leap
I've tried falling slow-motion into the ocean
and counting the fish in the deep

But I can't seem to slip into sleep
I've tried both the heavenly and earthly approach
cloud-counting star-counting grass-counting
pebble-counting
I've even tried counting with humming:
> *'Ten green bottles standing on the wall*
> *Ten green bottles . . .'*
But no, I don't accidentally fall
with the green ones in a heap

At last – I give up in defeat
I just know I'll never slip into s
              s
               s
                s
                 z
                  z
                   z
                    l
                     l
                      l
                       e
                        e
                         e
                          e
                           p

In The Great Womb-Moon

In the great womb-moon
I once did swoon

Time was a millennium
In my mother's belly

There was water
There was tree
There was land
There was me

Time was a millennium
In my mother's belly

There was planet
There was star
There was light
There was dark

Time was a millennium
In my mother's belly

How I frog-kicked
And I frolicked
Like a cosmic
Little comic . . .

Then came a century, the waters subsided,
I was forced out like a morning-star
Into the borders of another world.
I'm not unhappy, but sometimes,
There's a wee mourn in me for the time when —

Time was a millennium
In my mother's belly

Carnival-Time

'Look how they coming, Mummy,
Big-storm down the street,
Look how they coming like palm trees
Come to wave in London,
The music itching me feet
The music itching me feet

Look how they moving, Mummy,
movements wicked in the street,
look how they heaving and weaving
like rhythm come to shake-up brick houses –
The music itching me feet
The music itching me feet

Look how they flowing, Mummy,
river-rippling down the street,
Look how they gliding like boat-of-flames,
come to light-up river Thames –
The music itching me feet
The music itching me feet

Look at Bearman and Beastman bouncing
Look at the Dragon-Lady, how she flouncing,
Look at Humming-bird girl how...'

'Boy, you full of poetry, but no-way, no-way
you ain't jumping in no band today –
Not until you finish that homework, hear what I say.'

Tube-Trapped

Can't move forward
Can't move back –
We're underground
Stuck on the tracks

And the minutes
Ticking by –
Slow as the hands
Of an octopus

Wish I'd taken
Time to have
Some breakfast
Or even a snack

Guess I'm really
Tube-trapped
Just another sardine
Squeezed into the pack

And today's the day Mum's forgotten
To slip an apple in my rucksack.

When My Friend Anita Runs

When my friend Anita runs
she runs straight into the headalong –
legs flashing over grass, daisies, mounds.

When my friend Anita runs
she sticks out her chest like an Olympic
champion – face all serious concentration.

And you'll never catch her looking around,
until she flies into the invisible tape
that says, she's won.

Then she turns to give me
this big grin and hug

O to be able to run like Anita,
                    run like Anita,
Who runs like a cheetah.
If only, just for once, I could beat her.

Sea-Rock

Sea rock us to love
      rock us to love

Breeze glad us to touch
      glad us to touch

Sun shift us in strides
      shift us in strides

Trees keep the gold and green of memory
      keep the gold and green of memory

But most of all sea
      rock us to love
      rock us to love

Autumn Song

Rusty-red, yellow,
Brown
Summer's gone,
Winter to come

By the windfall of apples
And the stripping of trees
By the pick-up of conkers
And the carpet of leaves

By the tired-face flowers
And the mould on the mound
By the soles crunching berries
And the bees' farewell-hum

Rusty-red, yellow,
Brown
Summer's gone,
Winter to come

Tree-Money

Autumn
is tree-money
everywhere on the ground –
red, gold, brown.

Gull

The oil-stricken gull
has struggled ashore,
and although full-grown,
looks like a bewildered
scraggy fledgling.

Her oil-tarred wings
seem heavy as lead
as she totters slightly,
stiff-legged.

Staring out at us
with an unblinking
atomic,
almost comic surprise.

She hasn't taken any sides
but she's lost her natural home
and more. An unanswerable cry
is stuck in her throat
               Why?
                Why?
                   Why?

The Dissatisfied Poem

I'm a dissatisfied poem
   I really am
there's so many things
   I don't understand
like why I'm lying
   on this flat white page
when there's so much to do
   in the world out there
But sometimes when I catch a glimpse
   of the world outside
it makes my blood curl
   it makes me want to stay inside
and hide
   please turn me quick
before I cry
   they would hate it if I wet the pages

The Day They Turned The Clock Back

The day they turned the clock back
I nearly got a heart-attack

It looked so cold
It looked so dark

I knew my mother would say,
'No park'

I knew I couldn't stay out late,
Like summer when I played out till eight.

Snowflake

Snowflake
you little clown

c
a
r
n
i
v
a
l
l
i
n
g
d
o
w
n

A small ghost kiss
on my warm tongue.

Making My First Snowman
In My Mother's Pink Rubber Gloves

I scooped and shaped him lovingly,
I piled and patted best as could be,
though my pink hands were burning me,
I kept on building my first snowman.

I shaped his shoulders and fixed his neck,
I smoothed his face and rounded his head,
though my pink hands were freezing me,
I kept on building my first snowman.

I put the usual carrot in, for the nose,
a banana for a mouth, my two best conkers for
his eyes,
though my pink hands were killing me,
I kept on building my first snowman.

I threw my Dad's black jacket
to keep the cold from his back,
I stuck on his head the old felt hat,
then I stepped back.

Why was he staring at me with those big eyes?
Why was he so freezingly alive?
Man, why was he looking at me so?

                                    Oh, No,

He wasn't a snowman.
HE WAS A SNOWCROW!

Stormman

He snatches up
all the little winds
growing big
under the hood of his skin.

He bays at the skies
bringing down thunder
and lightning
on his side.

He works himself up
into a hunger-sucking rage.
With his whirring-eye
and his hurricane-style

With his flapping-fling
and that singeing-sting,
who can stop him
as he comes howling in?

A man werewolf
size like King Kong
so, Stormman comes
whittling down.

Picking up the waves he's raised
he bashes the sea-front,
throwing himself about further inland;
battering windows and doors;

Clawing up rooftiles;
and heaven help anything not secure
like dustbin covers!
Stormman just sends them flying like frisbees.

Getting up
in the middle of the night,
I reach to put on the light.
Suddenly –

Stormman knocks out Electricity,
sending me stumbling
back to bed
as if from a Bogey

By morning
all worn-out
a limp thing –
he crawls out back to sea.

But look at the debris.
Look at the countless fallen trees.
The harvest of shambles,
Signing his name everywhere –

STORMMAN WOZ ERE

Hail Me!

I ping-ponged
on the rooftops
I spin-spun
in the gutters
I bounced down
on the concrete
I hit upon
the flowers
I rolled off
the edges
of window-ledges
and hedges

I lay around
for as long as I could
little ice-bullets –
then I vanished.

Weather-Moan

How it kyan snow so
How it kyan cold so
How it kyan fog so
How it kyan frost so
How it kyan rain so
How it kyan hail so
How it kyan damp so
How it kyan dark so

Is how it hard so?

Spell To Bring Out Back The Sun

Banana of my life
Golden-delicious of my eye

Crisp in the crunch
Jewel in the crown

Flounder in the sea
The beesknee – the beesknee

Sun, come out and play
your yellow symphony.

Grown-Up Parties

I love having parties
but not my Mum
as soon as the invites have gone
she begins to look glum –
fretting and regretting,
pacing up and down –

Elizabeth – a carnivore
Henry – allergic to cheese
Valerie – a calorie-counter
Mira – gluten free

On the day of the party
always the same old confusion –
Dad chopping up the onions
tears streaming down his cheeks,
just misses chopping his finger
as Mum gloomily repeats:

Percival – now vegan
Susan – can sense if it's organic
Paul – at least I think it's Paul,
he hates the taste of garlic

Grown-up parties!
Why can't she just give them –
crisps and ice-cream and smarties.

Dream-Lady

Old-Lady, Dream-Lady
carrying your home around
in a supermarket trolley

Pushing it lopsided
right down the middle
of the traffic

Like an own-way crab
on wheels,
trying to steer it clear,

Horns honk
heads peer
but Old-Lady, Dream-Lady
gives it all an indifferent stare

She's heading
for the big furniture store.
She's heading to set up home
Soon as the doors are closed –

To wrap herself once more
in her cardboard world of dreams.

Listening To A Tale About A Mum And Dad

Dad has given up smoking.
Mum has not.
They quarrel a lot.

Every time Mum lights up
Dad throws open the window
As if to get rid of a fog.

'You're polluting the place,' he says.
Mum gives him a glare,
And goes on puffing like an engine anyway.

Then Dad who's lost his job says,
'You'll die of lung cancer,'
'Like hell I will,' Mum puffs back in answer.

I sit through it
As though I'm dumb
What will become of Dad and Mum?

Give Yourself A Hug

Give yourself a hug
when you feel unloved

Give yourself a hug
when people put on airs
to make you feel a bug

Give yourself a hug
when everyone seems to give you
a cold-shoulder shrug

Give yourself a hug –
a big big hug

And keep on singing,
'Only one in a million like me
Only one in a million-billion-thrillion-zillion
like me.'